Property of:
Lower Richland High School

D1361599

MALCOLM X
Fighting for Human Rights

MALCOLM X
Fighting for Human Rights

Jeff Burlingame

Enslow Publishing
101 W. 23rd Street
Suite 240
New York, NY 10011
USA

enslow.com

Published in 2018 by Enslow Publishing, LLC.
101 W. 23rd Street, Suite 240, New York, NY 10011

Copyright © 2018 by Jeff Burlingame

Library of Congress Cataloging-in-Publication Data

Names: Burlingame, Jeff, author.
Title: Malcolm X : fighting for human rights / Jeff Burlingame.
Description: New York, NY : Enslow Publishing, [2018] | Series: Rebels with a cause | Includes bibliographical references and index. | Audience: Grades 7–12.
Identifiers: LCCN 2016057563 | ISBN 9780766085190 (library bound : alk. paper)
Subjects: LCSH: X, Malcolm, 1925-1965—Juvenile literature. | Black Muslims— Biography—Juvenile literature. | African American civil rights workers— Biography—Juvenile literature.
Classification: LCC E185.97.L5 B85 2017 | DDC 320.546092 [B] —dc23
LC record available at https://lccn.loc.gov/2016057563

Printed in the United States of America

To Our Readers: We have done our best to make sure all website addresses in this book were active and appropriate when we went to press. However, the author and the publisher have no control over and assume no liability for the material available on those websites or on any websites they may link to. Any comments or suggestions can be sent by e-mail to customerservice@enslow.com.

CONTENTS

INTRODUCTION

Malcolm Little's sleep was peaceful, but what woke him was anything but: chaos, punctuated by gunshots, his father's angry shouts, and the rest of his family's terrifying screams as they saved his four-year-old life by pulling him from his bed and rushing him outside. Through the orange flames that surrounded them. Through the thick smoke that rendered their eyes useless and clogged their lungs.

Outside, in the middle of the chilly autumn darkness in Lansing, Michigan, Malcolm's family huddled together and watched their home burn. Inside, the sound of an explosion cut through the flames. The farmhouse was destroyed. Malcolm later described what he recalled of the incident. He said,

> We were lunging and bumping and tumbling all over each other trying to escape. My mother, with the baby in her arms, just made it into the yard before the house crashed in, showering sparks. I remember we were outside in the night in our underwear, crying and yelling our heads off.[1]

Malcolm X survived a childhood full of traumatic events to become one of the most well-known civil rights leaders of all time.

The destruction Malcolm saw on November 7, 1929, haunted him for the rest of his life. He often talked about the event. In his autobiography, Malcolm discussed the fire—and whom he believed had caused it—in more detail. He wrote: "I remember being suddenly snatched awake into a frightening confusion of pistol shots and shouting and smoke and flames. My father had shouted and shot at the two white men who had set the fire and were running away."[2]

Malcolm's version of what happened next has been disputed over the years. As Malcolm told it, "[W]hite police and firemen came and stood around watching as the house burned down to the ground."[3] Others say the firefighters refused to come to help put out the blaze because the house was outside their jurisdiction and therefore not their fire to fight.[4] But by everyone's account, Malcolm's contention that the police were not completely helpful to his family was correct. In fact, when officers arrived on the scene, they arrested Malcolm's father, Earl Little, for illegal possession of a gun and suspicion of arson. They believed the father had intentionally set his own house on fire.[5]

> **"I remember being suddenly snatched awake into a frightening confusion of pistol shots and shouting and smoke and flames."**

Earl Little did have what could have been interpreted as a motive for setting the fire. Shortly before his house burned to the ground, he had been told that his family would have to move. Several of his white neighbors were against having a black family living in their neighborhood. To get them to leave, they had argued that Little's purchase of the house had been illegal. They pointed to the home's deed, which read: "This land shall never be rented, leased, sold to, or occupied by … persons other than those of the Caucasian race."[6]

At the time, many facets of life in the United States were subject to racial segregation. Frequently, African Americans were not allowed to attend certain schools, eat at certain restaurants, or, as in this case, live in certain neighborhoods. Those living in Lansing's all-white community especially did not want a black family that was led by a person as controversial as Earl Little in their neighborhood.

Little, a Baptist minister, was an outspoken and controversial man. He was a devotee of another black man, Marcus Garvey, who was the head of the Universal Negro Improvement Association (UNIA), a movement that called upon blacks to be proud of their heritage and to become independent from whites. Although slavery had been abolished in the United States several decades earlier, Garvey and his followers believed that, in many ways, blacks still were enslaved to white people. He also felt that blacks never would be treated equally in America, so they should come together and return to Africa, which he believed to be their homeland. Little was one of Garvey's biggest supporters. This made him a target of white supremacist groups, such as the Ku Klux Klan. Whites saw Little as a troublemaker and frequently harassed him.

According to Malcolm, the fire was not the first time angry whites had seriously attacked his family. Most of the time, his defiant father stood up against his harassers and fought back. This time, there would be no fighting back. The house was destroyed, and the Little family had to salvage whatever belongings they could from the charred remains and find a new place to live.

Unfortunately, life had several more traumatic times left for Malcolm to experience. When they happened, Malcolm internalized every moment of despair and every tragic circumstance. He gathered ideas from his father, from Garvey, and from the many other outspoken black men he would meet along the way. Life's lessons turned Malcolm Little into a controversial, defiant, and rebellious man with strong opinions as to the way black people should act. He had equally strong opinions of the white man who he felt held black people down. Life's lessons turned Malcolm Little into Malcolm X. There would come a time when almost everyone in the United States would know—and many, even fear—that name.

1

On the Move

nger and violence reigned in the world Malcolm Little was born into on May 19, 1925. Much of that hostility occurred right inside his own home. His parents, Earl and Louise, fought over almost everything. Oftentimes, the couple fought over the inability of Earl Little to put food on the table. He worked as a manual laborer—and was often unemployed—but preaching was his passion. But passion did not pay the bills. Earl and Louise Little may have come from dissimilar backgrounds, but they already had been married six years by the time Malcolm was born. It often seemed as if that marriage would not make it another day.

Poorly educated, Earl Little followed—and later taught—the beliefs of Marcus Garvey. Garvey was a charismatic leader born in Jamaica who believed blacks should unite and return to their homeland of Africa, where they could rule their own nation without the influence of oppressive whites. Garvey even created a fleet of freight ships called the Black Star Line to help transport those of African descent to Africa. Garvey's speeches helped feed into the resentment many blacks in the United States had for white men. He even started his own militia.

Earl Little was president of the Omaha, Nebraska, branch of the UNIA. When Malcolm was born, Garvey

Malcolm X was born Malcolm Little. He was the seventh child of his father, Earl, and the fourth child of his mother, Louise.

was no longer leading the UNIA because he recently had been placed in prison for mail fraud. Little had desperately tried to get Garvey released from jail and had sent several letters asking for his release. He even sent one, dated June 8, 1927, to the president of the United States, Calvin Coolidge. None of Little's efforts helped. Garvey soon was deported back to his home country of Jamaica. Even so, Little continued to preach Garvey's controversial message, and he traveled to various cities to spread word about the UNIA to other blacks.

Marcus Garvey was a Jamaican-born black nationalist. Both of Malcolm's parents followed his teachings.

Malcolm's mother was a follower of Garvey as well and believed in fighting for black rights. However, in nearly every other respect she was the opposite of her husband. Louise Little was raised on the Caribbean island of Grenada and had a high-school education, which made her one of the better educated black women of her day. She had a black mother and a white father, which had left her with a light skin tone that often led people to believe she was white. She met Earl Little in Montreal, Canada, and married him in 1919. It was Earl Little's second marriage. His first one had ended in divorce after he walked out on his wife and their three children.[1]

A Turbulent Childhood

Malcolm was his father's seventh child, and his mother's fourth. Like his mother, Malcolm also was born with light skin. His parents sometimes favored him over his older siblings—which included brothers Wilfred and Philbert and sister Hilda—because of this, but that did not mean Malcolm was treated well. The opposite was true, in fact. Sometimes his mother would scrub his skin with a brush to try to make it even lighter. Other times, his conflicted mother would send Malcolm outside to play in the sun to make his skin darker.

Then there were the beatings. Malcolm seemed to get less of them from his father than his siblings and his mother did, but he still got them. A majority of the time, when Malcolm was whipped, it came from his mother, who herself had been abused as a child.

But turmoil in Malcolm's life did not only come from inside his home. Because of his beliefs and his outspoken personality, Earl Little was the target of many white supremacists, who believed he was nothing but a trouble-maker. One often-repeated story says that while Malcolm still was in his mother's womb, his family's home was surrounded by several members of the Ku Klux Klan, who were wearing hoods, riding horses, and carrying guns.

Malcolm also said the Klansmen shattered every window in his family's house and then rode off into the night. Some family members, including Malcolm's mother, have said they doubt that incident happened.[2]

Whether or not the story was true, the Littles did leave Omaha soon after Malcolm was born. They briefly lived in Milwaukee, Wisconsin, and Albion, Michigan, before settling into an old, two-story farmhouse on the outskirts of Lansing, Michigan. Earl Little hoped he finally had found a place where his family might be safe from the persecution they had received because of the color of their skin. But the section of Lansing the Littles moved into was primarily white, and Earl Little continued to speak out for black empowerment and independence. Those two factors kept the peaceful life he desired out of Earl Little's reach.

When Malcolm was four years old, a group of white neighbors found a legal means to get the Littles to move. A clause in the deed to the Littles' home stated that no blacks could live on the property. The neighbors went to court to sue the Littles and won, forcing them to move. But Earl Little was defiant. He was determined to remain in the house he had bought and, not surprisingly, was willing to fight for it.

That turned out to be a bad decision. Two weeks after the court judgment, on November 7, 1929, the house caught fire in the middle of the night while the family was asleep, and it burned to the ground. Fortunately, the family escaped before anyone was injured. Malcolm and many historians blame a white supremacist group for starting the fire. However, authorities at the scene arrested Earl Little, thinking he may have deliberately set the blaze with the theory that if he could not have the house, then no one could. Charges against Little were later dropped.[3]

Their home in ruins, the Littles moved again. They eventually wound up a short distance away in East Lansing. Thanks in part to donations, Earl Little was able to purchase six acres of farmland and build a four-room house on the property. It sounds like a comfortable living situation, but actually it was not. The rural home did not have indoor plumbing and was poorly insulated, offering little protection from the chilly Michigan winters. The nine-member family made do. They used the large amount of land around them to raise their own food. They had chickens and rabbits and grew vegetables in their garden.

In 1931, Malcolm began kindergarten at Pleasant Grove Elementary School. He and his siblings were the only black children in the school, but they were treated well by their classmates. For a short time, the rural setting allowed the Littles to escape persecution from bigoted white people and live in a peaceful manner. But the violence that had plagued the family soon resumed.

A Devastating Death

Malcolm was a few months into his sixth year when the worst tragedy yet struck his family. On September 28, 1931, his father was found dying on some streetcar tracks in Lansing. Officials determined Earl Little had been

The Universal Negro Improvement Association once elected Marcus Garvey as provisional president of Africa.

accidentally run over by a streetcar. A newspaper account of his death reported the same thing.

In spite of the reports, some blacks believed Earl Little was attacked and brutally beaten by the Black

Legionnaires hate group, who then placed his body on the tracks where the streetcar ran him over. Malcolm also believed this version of the story. He had gone to many meetings with his father, had heard him preach the gospel of Garvey, and had seen the disdain many white folks had for Garvey, his father, and any black man who spoke out for equality. Whatever happened to Earl Little, he was barely clinging to life when he was found and taken to the hospital. He died shortly after he arrived there.

Authorities woke Malcolm's family in the middle of the night to deliver the news. For the Littles, the news was both emotionally and financially devastating. At the time, the United States was in the midst of the Great Depression, an era where work was difficult to come by and millions of people lost their jobs, homes, and savings because of it. For many people, finding a job during the Great Depression was nearly impossible.

Work was even harder to come by for blacks, especially black women with little or no work history. Louise Little found some odd jobs here and there to keep her family afloat. Her light skin helped her get cleaning jobs in homes of white people who might otherwise not have hired her. When she straightened her naturally curly hair, it was difficult for many people to tell she was black. Employers who discovered she was black or the widow of the outspoken Earl Little immediately fired her.

Malcolm's oldest brother, Wilfred, quit school and found odd jobs to also help the family. Still, Malcolm and his siblings often had little to eat. The family took handouts, and whatever money they got, they would

SAVED BY THE NEW DEAL

When the US stock market crashed on October 24, 1929, it set in motion a worldwide economic crisis that left millions of people jobless, homeless, and starving. The day that became known as "Black Thursday" in the United States, and the effects of the crash quickly traveled to Europe and other industrialized nations. The timing of the crash was horrible for farmers in the Midwest, because they also soon faced drought and severe dust storms—an event that was called the Dust Bowl—that destroyed their lands. Many farmers went looking for jobs elsewhere, but there were none to be found. Relief finally began when Franklin D. Roosevelt was elected president in 1932. President Roosevelt introduced a sequence of government programs designed to stimulate the economy. Still, the Great Depression did not end until the 1940s, when the United States entered World War II.

spread as far as they could, buying the cheapest ingredients and making them last. Malcolm recalled, "[T]here were times when there wasn't even a nickel and we would be so hungry and dizzy. My mother would boil a big pot of dandelion greens, and we would eat that … [C]hildren would tease us, that we ate 'fried grass.'" Despite the teasing, Malcolm remained a popular kid in school. Class photographs show a grinning boy who is a half-head taller than the next-tallest boy.

Louise Little eventually had to accept welfare benefits from the government. It was a humiliating concession for the once-proud woman, and it took a toll on her mental health. She did not like taking handouts. So she began to withdraw from society and, as Malcolm put it, would "talk to herself nearly all of the time now … Eventually my mother suffered a

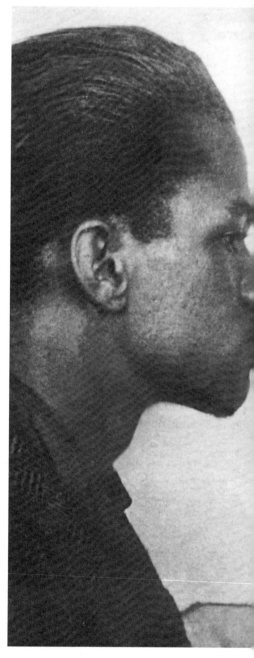

When Malcolm X was a teenager, he was arrested in Boston for larceny. These are the mug shots that were taken at the time.

complete [mental] breakdown, and the court orders were finally signed. They took her to the State Mental Hospital in Kalamazoo."[5] This happened on January 9, 1939. Louise Little lived there for the next twenty-six years.

By that point, the state already had declared Louise Little an unfit parent and had taken all but her oldest children away. Malcolm, now thirteen, was placed in the care of foster parents Mabel and Thornton Gohanna, who were paid to take in problem children. That is exactly what Malcolm had become. The tall, thin teenager who once had excelled in basketball, football, baseball, and boxing had taken to stealing food from the local store to help his family. He had been kicked out of school several times for misbehaving, although it was little surprise to anyone that he did so. He had lived a childhood that would be tough for anyone to come out of unscathed. His family had been attacked for the color of their skin. He had become sick from hunger. His father had died a controversial death. His mother had suffered a nervous breakdown. And there were many more tragedies Malcolm would endure.

After his mother was sent to the mental institution, Malcolm left the Gohannas' house and returned to his home, where Wilfred and Hilda had been allowed to remain to take care of the family household. Both worked hard to do so, with Wilfred taking on the role of father and Hilda becoming the acting mother. Hilda also tried to stay in school and took miscellaneous jobs when she could to help pay the bills.

Despite his older siblings' efforts, Malcolm did not live there long this time. In the fall of 1939, the state sent him to a juvenile detention home in the nearby small town of Mason, Michigan. The home was run by the Swerlein family. Malcolm liked the Swerleins, although he would later say the family only liked him "in the way they liked their house pets."[6]

A Place in the World

Malcolm attended Mason Junior High School, became class president, and received good grades for a while. As one of the only black students at the school, it was not long before he realized that being a black teen—even a well-liked black teen—had its limitations. For example, it was considered inappropriate for black boys to date white girls, although several of them reportedly had a crush on the handsome Malcolm. If Malcolm attempted to talk to a white girl, any white boys watching would browbeat him. Biographer Bruce Perry said Malcolm was the first person to be blamed when something was stolen at school, and he was not even allowed to get his hair cut in the town of Mason. Even the Swerleins called him names.

Malcolm was discouraged at how he was treated but tolerated it as well as could be expected; he was growing used to the abuse. Being treated differently from his white classmates made Malcolm long to find a place in the world. Did such a place even exist? He was talented in many ways, especially as a speaker, and one day he told an English teacher he would like to use that gift and become a lawyer to help down-and-out families like his. The teacher discouraged Malcolm, saying, "We all here like you, you know that. But you've got to be realistic about being a nigger. A lawyer—

that's no realistic goal for a nigger. You need to think about something you can be ... Why don't you plan on carpentry?"[7] The term nigger is a racial slur derived from the Latin word for black. Years later, Malcolm mentioned that believing what that teacher had told him was one of his biggest regrets.

> **As a young teenager, Malcolm X was discouraged by teachers who thought he would never amount to anything. His grades started to plummet.**

The teacher's discouraging suggestion had a huge impact on Malcolm. Why should he study when he could not be what he wanted to be anyway? Furthermore, what was the point of even going to school when he could become a laborer without an education? Both were valid questions that Malcolm began to think about. Soon, Malcolm's negative thoughts became a self-fulfilling prophecy. He stopped focusing on his studies, and began once again to cause trouble at school.

It became apparent that Malcolm might need another change of scenery. Surely, there was some place in the world for an intelligent, yet misguided, black teenager who was at a pivotal stage in his development. Then, when Malcolm was fifteen, he found one.

2

Growing Up on the Streets

Malcolm first visited his half-sister, Ella Collins, in the summer of 1940 at her home in a well-respected neighborhood of Boston, Massachusetts. Earl Little had fathered Ella along with three other children with his first wife. After the short visit during which he met many of his relatives for the first time, Malcolm returned to Michigan, went back to school for a short while, and then dropped out. What he planned to do next was anyone's guess, but a letter from Collins helped make his decision a lot easier. It read:

> *Dear Malcolm … I don't know how to write to you. But I will try … Sas lives in the mailbox looking for a letter from you. Gracie thought maybe you would be back by now. I know better. I had one of those long nightmares & dreams about you last nite. In fact, every nite since you left. We miss you so much … [E]verything seems dead here … I would like for you to come back but under one condition—Your mind is made up.[1]*

Collins wrote the letter in 1941 to make sure Malcolm was serious about the request he had made to her. Malcolm asked his sister if he could permanently come

Malcolm X's sister, Ella Collins (*pictured*), allowed Malcolm to come live with her in Boston in 1941.

live with her. But Collins could not take becoming attached to her young brother again, as she had the previous summer, only to have him leave once more. She loved her younger brother from the first time she met him when he was six years old, in 1931 at their father's funeral. She believed her little brother was unique. The admiration was mutual.

Moving to Boston

Malcolm took his sister up on her offer to come to Boston, and moved there permanently in 1941. They lived in a mostly black, middle-class area known by locals as the "Hill." The Hill was located next to Roxbury, the black ghetto section of Boston. The streets around Malcolm's new home were filled with blacks; it was unlike anything Malcolm had seen before. All his life Malcolm had been surrounded by white people—from his schoolteachers and his classmates to the social workers that frequently came to check on his mother and the rest of his family. Now, there were so many people that looked just like him, mingling through the area with purpose and a sense of belonging—exactly what Malcolm wanted for himself. It did not take long for him to begin to feel comfortable in his new environment. But that familiarity did not come exactly the way his half sister had wanted it to. Collins had hoped Malcolm would hang out in the Hill area, where the more-upstanding blacks lived. But Malcolm believed the Hill residents acted as if they were better than he was. So instead of hanging out there, he ventured off to Roxbury.

The streets of Roxbury were filled with hustlers—people who would use any means necessary to acquire goods or money. They would gamble, steal, and deal drugs. Malcolm's formal education may have ended back in Michigan, but his street education began in Roxbury. The hustlers were his new teachers.

Malcolm X became known as "Red" for his red-tinted hair.

Malcolm got a job shining shoes at Roxbury's trendy Roseland State Ballroom, where he met many famous musicians, such as Count Basie and Duke Ellington. When he was not working, Malcolm enjoyed dancing at the popular venue. Like many of Roxbury's blacks, Malcolm began wearing a flashy type of clothing called a zoot suit, which featured baggy, high-waisted pants pegged at the ankle, with a long jacket worn over it all. He often wore a matching hat. Malcolm soon earned a nickname on the streets of Roxbury: "Red," after his red-tinted hair, which he began to conk, or slick down with a substance called congolene.

Malcolm soon began hanging out with "Shorty," a man whose real name was Malcolm Jarvis. Shorty was

Swing dancing, like this couple is doing here at the Savoy Ballroom in Harlem, New York, was a popular pastime in bars Malcolm X frequented in both Harlem and in Boston.

also from Lansing, and he became Malcolm's mentor. Soon, the two became partners in crime, hanging out in Roxbury's pool halls and dive bars. Just sixteen, Malcolm was too young to legally be allowed into those bars, but he was tall, sharply dressed, and looked much older than his age, so it was no problem for him to get in. Shorty and Malcolm also were drinking alcohol, gambling, smoking marijuana, and, soon, committing burglaries.

Collins was not pleased with her brother. She had brought him from Michigan to Boston to free him from his life of poverty and to give him an opportunity to make something positive of his life. She spent a lot of time pushing him to become a better person and attempting to mold him into the successful man she knew he could be. But it seemed as if her efforts were wasted. Malcolm preferred hanging out with his friends in Roxbury rather than spending time with his family and the people on the Hill. His sister did not agree.

Collins did not give up hope for her brother. She helped to get Malcolm another job serving ice cream and sodas at a drugstore soda fountain. One of Malcolm's regular customers was a black girl named Laura who lived across the street. She was a year older and a high-school honor student. Malcolm was attracted to her innocence, and the two teens soon became a couple. They would go dancing at the Roseland, and Malcolm even brought her home to meet his sister, who approved of her. Collins must have been disappointed, then, when Malcolm took Laura home early after an evening of dancing at the Roseland so he could return to the ballroom to meet a different young woman, a well-dressed white girl named Beatrice. For a black man at the time, there was a certain coolness to be dating a white woman, and Malcolm showed Bea off every chance he got. As fast as she had come into Malcolm's life, Laura was out of it.

For various reasons, Collins did not like Bea. She wanted to get Malcolm away from his new girlfriend

This photo shows Harlem, New York in 1948. When Malcolm X moved there, he felt this black section of New York City was similar to the Roxbury section of Boston, where he had come from.

and away from the rest of the crowd they were running with. So she helped him get a job as a kitchen worker on a railroad. Malcolm did not want to do it at first but decided to take the job because it allowed him to travel to the biggest cities on the East Coast, including Washington, DC; Baltimore, Maryland; and Philadelphia, Pennsylvania. Malcolm also often made the four-hour trek to New York City.

Malcolm fell in love with New York on his first visit there. He was especially fond of the black area of the city, Harlem, which he found similar to Boston's Roxbury district, only bigger and more exciting. Harlem was alive, full of black men and women fully participating in life. The streets were full of blacks of all social classes. Down-on-their-luck prostitutes lived in Harlem. So did rich doctors. Malcolm was inspired by the latter, but he also was disappointed that, even in the 1940s, the well-off blacks were not allowed to live in some of the city's more upper-class neighborhoods. Malcolm was seeing firsthand what his father and Marcus Garvey had said: blacks often were treated as inferior by whites. Malcolm, in fact, believed the opposite to be true, that whites were the inferior species.

But that did not mean Malcolm thought blacks were perfect. He believed their biggest weakness came from trying to act white. He also told one interviewer:

There is plenty wrong with Negroes. They have no society. They're robots, automations. No minds of their own ... They are a black body with a white brain. Like the monster Frankenstein ... At the bottom on the social heap is the black man in the big-city ghetto. He lives night and day with the rats

STILL STRUGGLING

In the 1920s and 1930s, an African-American political and cultural movement began in Harlem, New York, the ideas of which influenced many other areas both in the US and worldwide. Called the Harlem Renaissance, the movement inspired artists, writers, musicians, politicians, philosophers, and others to focus on issues affecting African Americans in a way that would alter public perception about the race and also help promote civil rights.

Even after slavery was abolished, life in the South was still difficult for blacks. African Americans still were treated like second-class citizens and faced poverty and discrimination on a daily basis. They expressed their frustrations, shed light on the injustices, and sought to demonstrate their humanity through music, art, and literature. Jazz music became the sound track of the movement through such artists as Louis Armstrong, Billie Holiday, and Duke Ellington. Novels, drama, and poetry depicting black life gained popularity. Notable writers of the period include Langston Hughes, Zora Neale Hurston, and Claude McKay. The Harlem Renaissance set the stage for the civil rights movement of the 1960s.

and cockroaches and drowns himself with alcohol and anesthetize[s] himself with dope, to try and forget where and what he is. That Negro has given up all hope.[2]

The Streets of Harlem

Still, as an uneducated black man, it was not those professionals with whom Malcolm would associate when, in the spring of 1943, he lost his railroad job, left his sister's house in Boston, and moved to Harlem. He was back hanging out with the same type of crowd he had before. He found a job as a waiter in a bar called Small's Paradise. Small's was a hot spot for well-dressed businessmen who liked to enjoy a cocktail or two after work. It also was a hot spot for first-rate hustlers and thugs, the likes of which Malcolm had never seen. If what he learned in Roxbury had been his high school, Harlem was his university. Malcolm would learn a lot there, especially from those who frequented Small's. Most of what he learned was not positive, including how to be paid to find prostitutes for the men who were looking for them. That skill led to his eventual firing from Small's when, one day, he agreed to find a prostitute for one of the bar's customers. The customer was an undercover police officer. Malcolm was not arrested, but he did lose his job. Now, instead of simply supplementing his income with the petty crimes he was committing, those crimes became Malcolm's only source of income—and the source of a lot more trouble.

Malcolm became "Detroit Red" on the streets of Harlem, to help distinguish him from the other "Reds" in the area. As he had done in Boston, Malcolm began selling drugs. The money he made doing so paid for his own drug and gambling habits. Malcolm had been smoking marijuana and drinking alcohol for a while, but in Harlem he began using harder drugs, such as heroin and cocaine. He said he smoked marijuana, popularly known at the time as "reefer," day and night.

Even though Malcolm may have felt intelligent and invincible, he actually was anything but. His drug deals and robberies had left him somewhat paranoid, and he moved from motel to motel to keep from being caught. Police were said to always be on the lookout for him, although Malcolm also said some of those police ignored his activity. He said,

> *I had a good working system of paying off policemen … I had several men working and I was a steerer myself. I steered white people with money from downtown to whatever kind of sin they wanted in Harlem. I didn't care what they wanted, I knew where to take them to it … [And] my best customers always were the officials, the top police people, businessmen, politicians and clergymen.*[3]

Malcolm's feelings about white people changed throughout his life. In his youth, he had wanted to be white, as he thought that was the only way he could become successful. As he grew, he began to hate white people for the way he felt they treated blacks like second-class citizens. He was not the only black person who felt that way. When Malcolm was coming of age, racial tensions were high across the entire United States. In areas where there were large numbers of blacks, such as Harlem, they were especially so.

Shortly after Malcolm arrived in Harlem, a white police officer shot and wounded a black soldier who reportedly had taken offense to the language the officer had used with a black woman he was arresting. False rumors quickly began to spread that the white cop had killed the black soldier. Thousands of blacks rioted in the streets, looting stores and other buildings. The military was called in to help the city's police force gain control, and fifteen hundred civilians were enlisted to help, as well. In the end, five people were killed, four hundred were injured, and five hundred people, all black, were arrested.[4]

Property damages were estimated at $5 million.[5]

After Malcolm had committed a series of robberies with his friend and accomplice Sammy McKnight, he sensed it was time to get out of town for a while to take some of the heat off him. So he headed back to Boston. His old

The Harlem Riot of 1943 left the shops and streets of the area in shambles.

girlfriend, Bea, was now married to a man who was away in the military, but this did not stop Malcolm from seeing her again. He also reunited with his mentor, Shorty, and resumed his life of crime on the streets.

After Malcolm turned eighteen years old in 1943, he was afforded another opportunity to get off the streets and to begin living a lawful life. The United States Army, still in the throes of World War II, tried to bring him into its ranks. Malcolm did not want to go to war. Long known by his peers as a joker, Malcolm devised a plan. On the day he was called into the army's recruiting office in Manhattan, he put on his zoot suit and his yellow shoes. The moment he walked in, he began acting strange. When he was brought in to see the army psychiatrist, he continued his act. Constantly looking around the room as if he were paranoid about being spied on, Malcolm stood up from his seat and whispered in the doctor's ear: "Daddy-o, now you and me, we're from up North here, so don't you tell nobody ... I want to get sent down South. Organize them nigger soldiers, you dig? Steal us some guns, and kill us crackers!"[6]

The army did not let Malcolm in. Thanks to some good acting, Malcolm was again free to work the streets—until the law finally caught up with him.

That happened in Boston in early 1946. In the city where his sister had brought him to help better his life, Malcolm had become the leader of a small burglary ring that included Shorty, Bea, and her sister. On January 12, Malcolm entered a jewelry story to pick up a stolen watch he had left there to be repaired. The store's owner was suspicious and summoned police, who arrived and arrested Malcolm. Malcolm surrendered willingly, and was fully cooperative in the ensuing investigation. He told the arresting officer about the loaded gun he was carrying. When questioned about a string of burglaries the police believed he had been involved in, Malcolm admitted to all of them. He even ratted out his fellow conspirators to receive a lighter sentence by being cooperative. It did not work out that way.

Malcolm's bail was set at ten thousand dollars. He could not pay it, so he had to remain in jail while he awaited trial, which was held in February. At the trial, the three white girls who had been arrested with Malcolm were seated at a table, while Malcolm and Shorty watched the proceedings from inside a locked cage. Malcolm had no lawyer, and received a steep sentence of eight to ten years in prison. The normal sentence for such crimes would be two or three years in prison, but Malcolm had a prior arrest, and the women involved in the robbery had said he forced them to participate. Shorty received the same sentence as Malcolm. Still, Malcolm felt he was treated unfairly because of his skin color and the fact that he had been running around with white women.

His observations led Malcolm to distrust the American justice system and the white people who ran it even more. During his time in prison, that distrust would continue to grow.

3

A New Name

On the streets of Roxbury, they had known Malcolm as "Red," and in Harlem he had been known as "Detroit Red." But Malcolm lost his nicknames and past identities in February 1946 when he arrived at Boston's Charlestown State Prison. In this dark place of confinement, Malcolm was just a number: 22483.

Built in 1805, Charlestown was the oldest state prison in Massachusetts, and the facility certainly showed its age. In fact, the prison had once been in such bad shape that it had been shut down, only to be reopened a short time later when another prison grew too crowded. Malcolm's cell was dirty and tiny, and had no running water. His toilet was a bucket in the corner.

On the streets, Malcolm had become addicted to cocaine. Without it, he was a cranky man who caused trouble almost from the moment he arrived at the prison. He was mean to everyone he encountered, including guards and fellow inmates. This earned him a lot of time in solitary confinement.

Malcolm did not learn from his stints in solitary. He continued being belligerent, and he spoke so negatively about organized religion that people began calling him "Satan." Malcolm had been raised in a religious household, but during his time in Boston and Harlem, he had lost all

Malcolm arrived in this building, the Charlestown State Prison in Massachusetts, in February 1946.

connection to religion. If there was a god, where was he when Malcolm needed his help? Prisoner Malcolm became a nonbeliever and even made fun of those who did believe. He got along with no one.

Malcolm's family had not given up on him, despite his rebellious ways. Ella Collins was his first visitor at Charlestown, and later recalled what it was like seeing her younger brother behind bars: "It was not a very pleasant

41

visit. Malcolm was as jive-talking, cocky, and unrepentant as ever. He showed no remorse or concern about family anxiety and seemed to believe that his only problem was being caught, that the next time he would be a smarter hustler. When I left … I was as upset as I had ever been with him."[1]

The same type of hustling Malcolm participated in on the streets also took place in prison, only with subtle differences. For example, Malcolm arranged bets for other prisoners, and he used ingredients from the kitchen to mix a crude cocktail that would get him high.

Over time, Malcolm calmed, mostly thanks to his meeting of a fellow inmate named John Elton Bembry. Bembry, better known by the nickname of Bimbi, was a well-respected, older black man. Bimbi and Malcolm met when Malcolm bumped into him in the prison yard, looking to start something. But the two men eventually became friends, and the well-read Bimbi encouraged Malcolm to read some books, too. Educate yourself, Bimbi told him. Malcolm resisted at first but then gave in. Soon, he was reading everything he could find in the prison library. He also began to educate himself in other ways, such as by taking correspondence classes in English and in Latin. To learn new words, Malcolm would obsessively copy them out of the dictionary onto a piece of paper.

Reading opened Malcolm's mind and showed him there were other ways of thinking far different from what he believed or had been taught. He could not get enough of books. In fact, the hours he spent reading in the dim light of his prison cell weakened his eyesight and caused Malcolm to need glasses. He got a pair of horn-rimmed ones. The studious look those glasses gave him became one of Malcolm's defining characteristics for years to come.

In January 1947, Malcolm was transferred to another Massachusetts prison, the Concord Reformatory. Prisoners were transferred for various reasons, and it was a common practice to do so. Malcolm even used his newfound love for reading and learning to help himself receive one such transfer. When he learned a prison in Norfolk, Massachusetts, had an experimental program that focused on helping reform prisoners and offered them more freedoms than both Charleston and Concord, Malcolm—with the help of his sister—applied for admission. In February 1948, he was accepted into the program and transferred to the Norfolk Prison Colony. The facility there was state of the art, as far as prisons go, and had a large library.

Various members of Malcolm's family continued to write him letters, and one from his brother Reginald helped change Malcolm's life forever. In the letter, Reginald told his brother to stop eating pork and smoking cigarettes to keep his body pure. This would help get him out of prison.

Malcolm did not understand how these seemingly random things would lead to his release, but he followed his brother's instructions. When Reginald later came for a visit, Malcolm began to understand. Reginald, and several other members of Malcolm's family, had joined a religious movement called the Nation of Islam.

Introduction to the Nation of Islam

Founded in Detroit, Michigan, in 1930, the Nation of Islam was modeled after Islam, an ancient religion that began in the Middle East. The millions of people across the world who follow Islam are called Muslims. Muslims believe God—or Allah, as they call him—revealed all his knowledge to a prophet named Muhammad, who then began preaching the word of the Koran, the holy book of the Muslims. Nation of Islam followers were called Black Muslims.

When Malcolm was introduced to the Nation of Islam, the movement's leader was a small black man named Elijah Muhammad. Muhammad, born October 7, 1897, in Sandersville, Georgia, was the son of former slaves. His birth name was Elijah Poole, and he changed his last name to Muhammad after he joined the Nation of Islam in 1931. He became leader in 1934, and the number of Black Muslims in the United States grew significantly under his control. Nation of Islam mosques sprung up across the country.

The principle beliefs of the Nation of Islam appealed to Malcolm. As one author put it, the black nationalist religious group placed a "strong emphasis on black pride, history, culture, and unity ... [and an] unblinking assertion that white men were devils, a belief that led Muhammad and his followers to advocate black separation from white society."[2]

At the core, the Nation of Islam's beliefs were similar to the message preached some two decades earlier by Marcus Garvey and his many followers—including Malcolm's father—that blacks needed to live separately from whites. Muhammad believed blacks were members of the powerful "original" race and were getting along well until they had been enslaved by whites. Many American blacks who believed they were being oppressed by the white man believed in the message of the Nation of Islam and became followers of Elijah Muhammad.

While he was incarcerated, Malcolm X became a devoted follower of Nation of Islam leader Elijah Muhammad.

Reginald used straight talk to sell his brother on the Nation of Islam:

> *You don't even know who you are … [T]he white devil has hidden it from you, that you are of a race of people of ancient civilizations, and riches in gold and kings. You don't even know your true family name, you wouldn't recognize your true language if you heard it … You have been a victim of the evil of the devil white man ever since he murdered and raped and stole you from your native land in the seeds of your forefathers.[3]*

Now twenty-three years old, Malcolm finally had his purpose in life. The teachings of the Nation of Islam and Elijah Muhammad spoke to him. He did believe that he had lived his life at the mercy of the white man who, in his mind, had constantly tried to keep him down. He thought about the time his teacher had told him he could not be a lawyer. He thought about how his family had been attacked by white supremacists. He thought about his father's death.

Malcolm spent every moment he could learning more about his new infatuation by reading as much as he could. One author said Malcolm was particularly affected by "the library's extensive collection of books and pamphlets about the captive Africans who had been taken to America in rat-infested ships, sold into slavery, and chained and whipped like miscreant dogs."[4] Such stories did nothing to improve Malcolm's already-negative attitude toward white people.

After he felt he had educated himself enough on the subject, Malcolm wrote a letter to Elijah Muhammad.

Elijah Muhammad is pictured here on the front page of his newspaper, *Muhammad Speaks.*

Muhammad wrote back, telling Malcolm he was not a criminal and should not be in jail. The real criminals, Muhammad said, were the whites who had made him commit the crimes in the first place, because he had no other way to succeed in the white man's world. The letter also included some money for Malcolm.

It was 1949 by the time Malcolm began following Muhammad's teachings. That same year, Malcolm began preaching them to anyone who would listen. In addition to the pork and cigarettes he already had relinquished, he swore off alcohol and drugs of any kind. He also practiced his public speaking by debating anyone he could on any subject at any time.

On March 23, 1950, Malcolm was transferred back to Charlestown State Prison because he refused to receive a shot that would protect him against Concord's contaminated water. He was now back in the same filthy prison where he had started serving his sentence. There, he spread the word of the Nation of Islam to every black prisoner he could. Soon Malcolm had earned a legendary status at Charlestown, and everyone wanted to talk about what he had done. Malcolm used each chance he had to chat with others as an opportunity to talk about Muhammad and the Nation of Islam.

In 1951, both Malcolm and his coconspirator, Shorty, went before the parole board, a group of people who have the power to let an inmate out of jail before he or she has served their entire sentence. The board decided to parole Shorty but not Malcolm. Thus, Malcolm stayed at Charlestown, and Shorty returned to Boston. The next year, Malcolm again came before the parole board. This time, his parole was granted, but certain conditions were placed on him. The most important one was that he had to show that he had a job waiting for him when he got out of prison. Malcolm's older brother Wilfred helped with that. Wilfred worked at a furniture store in Detroit and convinced his boss to hire Malcolm when he was released. Malcolm did not seem to mind that the store where he would be working made its money by preying on the poor, oftentimes blacks, selling cheap furniture to customers for inflated prices, and offering credit to those who needed it.

Prior to Malcolm's parole, his family had decided that Detroit would be a much better place for him to be than Boston. Malcolm was released from prison on August 7, 1952. He was twenty-seven years old and had spent six and a half years behind bars. Immediately after he was released, he went to stay the night at Collins's house before leaving for Detroit the next day. When he arrived there, Malcolm was a changed man. He had used prison as his personal seminary, or religious college, a place to study and master the teachings of Elijah Muhammad.

A New Life

Outside prison, Malcolm immediately began work on that new life. He joined the Nation of Islam's Temple Number One in Detroit and began attending meetings there. His devotion to the movement grew even stronger on August 31, when he and other members of the temple traveled to Chicago to see their leader speak in person. Of all the people at the event, Elijah Muhammad pointed to Malcolm and asked him to stand. Author Bruce Perry wrote: "The Messenger explained to the rest of the congregation that Malcolm had recently been released from jail. He described how faithfully Malcolm had corre-

Wilfred X, Malcolm X's brother (*left*), waits to speak at a Nation of Islam convention in Chicago, Illinois.

sponded with him from prison."[5] Muhammad told his followers, "I believe that he is going to remain faithful."[6] Muhammad soon drew Malcolm even closer under his wing. Malcolm's own words make it easy to understand why he became so faithful to Muhammad.

At this time, Malcolm also made a huge symbolic move to show his solidarity to the Nation of Islam and his disdain for white men. Shortly after joining the Detroit temple, Malcolm dropped his last name of "Little" and replaced it with an "X." His reasons were clear. He said:

The Muslim's "X" symbolized the true African family name that he never could know. For me, my "X" replaced the white slave-master name of "Little" which some blue-eyed devil named Little had imposed upon my paternal forebears. The receipt of my "X" meant that forever in the nation of Islam, I would be known as Malcolm X. Mr. Muhammad taught that we would keep this "X" until God Himself returned and gave us a Holy Name from His own mouth.[7]

Some years later, when Malcolm made a pilgrimage to Mecca, Saudi Arabia, the holiest city in Islam, he would replace the "X" with the last name "Shabazz."

Malcolm remained more than faithful to the cause, becoming one of its most-devoted followers. He fervently recruited members to his own temple, which helped him advance in power proportionally. By mid-1953, Malcolm had become the assistant minister of the Detroit temple. When Malcolm was off parole and thus able to leave Detroit, his minister there sent him to Boston to recruit members. Returning to the place where he had once been a criminal was a risky proposition for Malcolm. His sister and other family members had tried to keep him out of the city for fear the police there would only remember him as a criminal. But religion had changed Malcolm; he no longer worried about what the police would think because he knew he was not going to break any laws. He did talk with some of his old friends, but he avoided hanging out in the places he used to. He was now following the Nation of Islam's rules. Pool halls, alcohol, drugs, and even dancing were off limits.

Soon, Malcolm had recruited enough people to start a new temple in Boston. Appropriately, he became that temple's minister. It was the first of several head positions Malcolm would obtain over the next couple of years, as his tireless work for the Nation of Islam continued to be rewarded. His next leadership job came in Philadelphia in March 1954. Just two months later, Malcolm was named leader of Temple Number Seven in Harlem.

New York City's temple was only a storefront in a slum when Malcolm took over. But the potential for expansion in New York City was limitless. There were roughly one million blacks in the city, many of them poor and open to any message that might convince them that change was possible. The Nation of Islam certainly offered that hope.

Malcolm began promoting his temple, and membership slowly grew. Membership numbers also grew in Detroit and Boston and other cities, such as Pittsburgh, Pennsylvania; Atlantic City, New Jersey; Cleveland, Ohio; and Miami, Florida. The Nation of Islam was becoming a strong player in the national religious scene, but a majority of people in the United States still had not heard of the organization. One high-profile event that happened in April 1957 changed all that.

The event began in Harlem, when a white police officer beat a drunken black man who was involved in a fight on the streets. A crowd gathered to watch the incident. In the crowd was a Nation of Islam member named Johnson Hinton, who shouted at the police to stop their beating. Hinton said a policeman then attacked him as he was leaving the scene.[8] The policeman said he accidentally bumped into Hinton.[9] Whatever the truth, what happened next is indisputable.

Hinton was arrested and taken to jail. Word of his plight quickly made its way back to members of Hinton's temple, who gathered outside the police station in protest. Soon, Temple Number Seven's leader got word and joined the protest. Malcolm went inside the jail and demanded to see Hinton. By this point, thousands of blacks—temple members and others—had gathered outside. Malcolm told the police he would not tell the crowd to leave until he was allowed to see Hinton. The police finally allowed Malcolm to see the prisoner.

When he saw Hinton, Malcolm said later, "[I]t was all I could do to contain myself. He was only semi-conscious. Blood had bathed his head, face, and shoulders. I hope I never again have to withstand seeing another case of sheer police brutality like that … I told the lieutenant in charge, 'That man belongs in the hospital.'"[10] Fearing a riot, the police obliged and called an ambulance that took Hinton to the hospital. Much of the crowd marched through the streets behind the ambulance, all the way to the hospital. Others who were not originally involved joined in along the way.

At the hospital, the marchers gathered outside to wait to hear about Hinton's condition. When Malcolm came out and assured everyone that Hinton was receiving excellent medical care, the crowd left. Even the police were impressed by the power Malcolm had over such a large crowd of strangers. They could not believe one man could have so much control. From that time on, police were assigned to every scheduled speech Malcolm made to help with crowd control. Oftentimes, those speeches would draw thousands of people. Malcolm's words were usually defiant and always anti-white. Although it is often said that Malcolm was recommending violence, he was not. Malcolm did not advocate violence in and of itself; rather he advocated self-defense and self-protection—such as the right to bear arms—for himself, his family, and his fellow blacks. He felt they had the right to retaliate against injustices levied against them, by any means necessary. Where applicable, that included violence.

The Montgomery Bus Boycott

Then, on December 1, 1955, in Montgomery, Alabama, a woman named Rosa Parks would take a stand for civil rights. After finishing work as a seamstress at a department store, Parks hopped on Montgomery's Cleveland Avenue bus for her ride home. She took an empty seat in the fifth row, the first row of the "Colored Section" where blacks were allowed to sit. When a white male passenger came on board, Parks refused to give him her seat. At the time, it was customary for blacks to surrender their seats to whites. But Parks, who was a member of the National Association for the Advancement of Colored People (NAACP), would not. Parks was arrested for her defiance.

In protest of Parks's arrest, blacks were asked to boycott the Montgomery bus line and to refuse to ride any bus until black and white riders alike were treated equally. Tens of thousands of notes were sent out to places blacks frequented. The planned one-day boycott soon turned into a week, then a month, then a year. Without any black passengers, the bus line lost a lot of money. The months of negative media coverage was a huge public relations nightmare for the bus line. Eventually, the protest worked. On December 21, 1956, Montgomery's bus line was officially desegregated. Riders of any color now were allowed to sit wherever they wanted on Montgomery's buses.

Martin Luther King Jr. and Malcolm X disagreed in the use of violence to fight for civil rights.

SPEAKING OUT AGAINST RACIAL DISCRIMINATION

The Hinton incident was one of several high-profile situations where blacks in the United States stood up and spoke out against what they believed to be racial discrimination. Similar stances were being taken across the United States during what was called the civil rights movement. In America, the movement proper lasted from about the mid-1950s into the early 1970s, though its roots can be traced back to the late 1800s and early 1900s to separatist Booker T. Washington and to W. E. B. DuBois, who championed integration. Although these influential thinkers had different approaches of approaching the question of civil rights, their thoughts spawned a movement that Malcolm X and others would take up years later.

Rosa Parks was arrested for refusing to give up her bus seat to a white passenger on December 1, 1955, in Montgomery, Alabama.

The organization that planned the boycott was called the Montgomery Improvement Association. Leading that group was a black Baptist minister named Martin Luther King Jr., who soon would become a nationally known leader of the civil rights movement. King's approach to evoking change involved using calm, peaceful, and loving tactics. He did not believe in using violence to promote his cause, but rather nonviolent civil disobedience. King's beliefs differed vastly from Malcolm's angry and often-aggressive tactics.

4

Spreading the Word

Tall, attractive, and dark-skinned, Sister Betty Sanders was a member of the Nation of Islam's Harlem Temple who had adopted the letter X as her last name in 1956, shortly after she had met Malcolm. Betty X was studying to become a nurse, but according to Malcolm's autobiography, her schooling was about to end because her parents had discovered she was a Black Muslim and had threatened to cut her funding because of it.

Betty, who was twenty-three, seemed perfect for the thirty-two-year-old Malcolm. Despite these facts, Malcolm still had reservations for a couple of reasons. First, he had been rejected by several women in the past, and he was afraid another woman might tell him no. Malcolm did not want to deal with that personal rejection. Second, Malcolm felt it was necessary to gain approval from Elijah Muhammad before marrying. So he arranged for his mentor to meet Betty by flying her to Chicago to attend some classes there. Muhammad met her and approved of her. After all that, Malcolm decided to propose. Never the romantic type, Malcolm approached the proposal as if it were just another business deal he was conducting. He called her on the

Betty Sanders, later known as Betty Shabazz, married Malcolm X on January 14, 1958, in Detroit, Michigan.

phone and asked her if she wanted to get married, and she agreed. The marriage ceremony was conducted in much the same manner: as straightforward and quickly as possible. It happened on January 14, 1958, in Detroit.

That November, Betty gave birth to the couple's first daughter, Attallah. She and Malcolm would have five more daughters together. Qubilah was born in 1960; Ilyasah, named after Elijah Muhammad ["Ilyasah" is the feminine form of "Elijah"] was born in 1962; and Gamilah was born in 1964. In 1965, twins Malaak and Malikah were born.

The Newlyweds

The couple's first house was a humble two-bedroom place in Queens, New York. Malcolm had an office in the attic, and he would often spend large amounts of time in there reading, praying, and sometimes even sleeping. The house was owned by the Nation of Islam, and it was one of the many gifts the Nation provided to its top promoter. Malcolm also received a small amount of pay each week, a car, and travel expenses. The life he and Betty lived was far from extravagant.

The Nation of Islam also owned Muhammad's home in the South Side of Chicago, which was much nicer than Malcolm's. Muhammad's home was an eighteen-room Victorian mansion, and armed guards stood outside at all hours of the day. Muhammad and the Nation of Islam also operated several thriving businesses. They owned grocery stores, apartment buildings, and many other properties.

Malcolm did not look at the lifestyle discrepancies between himself and Muhammad as a problem. Malcolm

Malcolm X, holding his daughter Ilyasah, is interviewed by a reporter in New York in 1964.

was a very spiritual man and believed that his eternal life was far more important than whatever happened to him during the time he spent living on earth. He had no doubt the Nation of Islam would take care of him and his family, and that was all he desired. He still worked as hard as he could to spread the message of the Nation of Islam and Muhammad.

There are indications that Betty was not happy with the small amount of payment and possessions Malcolm was receiving for his tireless work. Despite his wife's concerns, Malcolm still was willing to submit to the sacrifice. In many ways, Muhammad was like the father that Malcolm had barely known. He also was Malcolm's mentor, and Malcolm would do just about anything to keep him happy and successful. In 1959, that meant becoming the Nation of Islam's ambassador and traveling across the world to spread the group's message. Malcolm's charisma and excellent public speaking skills gained him large audiences everywhere he went. People in other countries wanted to know what this Black Muslim uprising in the United States was all about. Muhammad appointed Malcolm to be the one to tell them.

Growing Attention

In addition to his using live speaking engagements to further his cause, Malcolm also began using the media. He began writing a weekly column for the *Los Angeles Herald-Dispatch* newspaper. His columns, like his speeches, were full of anti-white, pro-black Muslim propaganda. In one column, he wrote: "Our idea of 'heaven,' after being brainwashed by the white man's Negro puppets, (Negro preaches), seemed to revolve

Malcolm X holds up an issue of the *Muhammad Speaks* newspaper during a rally in New York City in 1963.

around INTEGRATION (Gen 6:2) and uniting (not with OUR OWN KING but) with the wicked race of white Christians who had kidnapped, robbed and enslaved us."[1]

When considered in context with the history of slavery, Malcolm's comments seem a lot less harsh. Black slaves from Africa were indeed treated poorly by whites and "kidnapped, robbed and enslaved," as Malcolm said they were. During what was called the Middle Passage portion of the slave ships' voyage to the United States, Africans were beaten, chained, and tortured. The conditions the black men, women, and children were placed under were so deplorable that many died of disease and starvation—and some took their own lives—long before they reached American shores. Even after the Emancipation Proclamation of 1863 freed slaves, and the Thirteenth Amendment to the Constitution in 1865 made slavery illegal in the United States, blacks still were not treated equally.

Malcolm's articles caused quite a stir in both black and white communities. In 1961, Malcolm helped found the Nation's own newspaper, called *Muhammad Speaks.* Each issue eventually was read by tens of thousands of people, and proceeds from newspaper sales funded Nation of Islam causes, such as building new temples and improving the ones that already existed. Malcolm also wrote for the newspaper. His basic message, as always, was black independence.

Television also helped spread the Nation of Islam's message. One TV show in particular played an enormous role in introducing the Nation to mainstream America. Called *The Hate That Hate Produced*, the show aired in July 1959. It was narrated by journalist Mike Wallace, who went on to become a legend in the broadcasting

Malcolm X met with controversial Cuban leader Fidel Castro in Harlem, New York, in 1960.

industry. The program was an in-depth look at the rise of the Nation of Islam, and it talked about the message of black supremacy that the Nation was trying to spread. It featured interviews with Muhammad and Malcolm X and showed scenes from well-attended Nation of Islam rallies across the United States. The program's title referred to the Nation of Islam's alleged "hate" for white people and the belief that it was a product of the hate that white people had for blacks.

The airing of the documentary on mainstream television had a huge impact on the country. Many white people became afraid of the movement. It also helped Malcolm become a well-known public figure across the United States. Malcolm basked in the spotlight his newly elevated status afforded him. He took pleasure in fielding questions from reporters and debating those whose opinions differed from his. Elijah Muhammad still was the leader of the Nation of Islam, but Malcolm had become its best-known spokesperson. This began to create tension between the two men.

The Nation of Islam's increased exposure introduced its teachings to more people, but with the growth came more negative scrutiny. The Federal Bureau of Investigation (FBI), which had opened a case file on Malcolm shortly after his release from prison and also had an open file on Martin Luther King Jr., took an even bigger interest in Malcolm's activities. The agency even hired members of the Nation of Islam to spy on him. What Malcolm did in September 1960 made the FBI pay even closer attention to what he was doing. That was the month Cuban leader Fidel Castro came to the United States to talk at the United Nations (UN) in New York City.

The United States was not on the best of terms with Cuba when Castro came to visit. Just one year earlier, the United States government had stood behind Castro as he led the charge to overthrow the dictatorship of Fulgencio Batista. However, after Castro came into power, some US leaders began to believe Castro was trying to turn his country into a Communist nation, similar to the Soviet Union. It was a path the United States did not want him to follow. In March 1960, President Dwight D. Eisenhower called for economic sanctions against Cuba, and he directed the Central Intelligence Agency (CIA) to begin planning the overthrow of Castro's regime. On September 26, Castro gave a speech denouncing the policies of the United States. The speech was the final straw for the United States, which severed all ties with Cuba in January 1961, and invaded the country in April.

Malcolm had very little contact with Castro during his visit to the United States. He met with the Cuban leader for just thirty minutes, at the celebrated Hotel Theresa in Harlem, where Castro had decided to stay after his delegation had been treated poorly at the more upscale Shelbourne Hotel in midtown Manhattan. However, those thirty minutes were enough for the FBI to take note of the visit and to place it into Malcolm's ever-growing file. By all accounts, Malcolm knew the FBI was monitoring him almost from the time the agency began doing so. That did not stop him from doing the same things he had been doing. Malcolm continued promoting the Nation of Islam, debating all comers, granting interviews, verbally attacking his enemies, and giving speeches across the country.

Meanwhile, Muhammad's health began to become an issue. It had been declining for some time, and he and his sons were starting to think about who would be the Nation's next leader. Malcolm had long been the Nation's number-two man, and, in 1962, had been awarded the title of national minister. Some in the Nation believed Malcolm already was, in everything but name, their leader.

> **Like Martin Luther King Jr., Malcolm X was of particular interest to the FBI, who monitored both civil rights leaders.**

Ronald Stokes

Soon, Malcolm himself began having his own problems with the leadership of Elijah Muhammad. One of them

AIR FRANCE FLIGHT 007

Malcolm did claim to have gained some revenge a little more than a month after the Stokes incident. That revenge came on June 3, 1963, when a group of Atlanta's upper-crust white citizens was flying back from a month-long tour of Europe, and their plane crashed shortly after taking off from Paris. The crash killed 130 people, and the people of Atlanta were devastated by the massive loss of life. However, Malcolm saw the crash as payback for what had happened to Stokes. In one speech, he called it "a very beautiful thing ...[God] really answered our prayers over in France."[2] This, of course, was a very troubling and divisive thing to say.

happened when Nation of Islam member Ronald Stokes was shot and killed by police on April 27, 1962, in Los Angeles. When that happened, it was Malcolm who flew to Los Angeles the next day to help keep the black public calm during the aftermath.

It was a dangerous and tricky political situation. Stokes was the secretary of the Los Angeles temple and worked at a dry cleaning business. On the day of the incident, suspicious police confronted Stokes and another worker as they were unloading clothes from a car. First, an argument, then a fight, broke out. A crowd gathered, more police arrived, and shots were fired. In the end, eight men had been shot: one police officer and seven Black Muslims. Stokes died at the scene. The patrol officer who shot him testified that Stokes had been unarmed but had "raised his hands in a menacing way."[3] *The Los Angeles Times* said the incident had been a riot by the Black Muslims, but it was never proven that any of them even had guns.[4] If that was true, Malcolm wondered, why was it necessary for police to use theirs? Malcolm believed so strongly in the innocence of his fellow Muslims because he knew what Stokes, and every other Muslim, had been trained on what to do if approached by police.

A photographer who was on the scene described what he saw. He said, "I arrived at the mosque in Los Angeles after the shooting took place, and there was great sadness amongst the people, you know. Malcolm was walking back and forth, shaking his head saying, 'They're going to pay for it, they're going to pay for it, they're going to pay for it, they're going to pay for it.'"[5] But Muhammad had told him not to commit any violence. So all Malcolm could do was hope for justice through the legal system. He did not get it. The officer who shot and killed Stokes was acquitted by a jury, and fourteen Black Muslims were tried for assault. Eleven of them were convicted and sent to prison.[6]

5
Leaving the Nation of Islam

E ach of the more than 250,000 people gathered at the Lincoln Memorial in Washington, DC, on August 28, 1963, shared a common goal: they were there to participate in the March on Washington for the Jobs and Freedom civil rights event. The event was scheduled to let the US government know its people wanted legislation passed that would ensure every American was treated equally, regardless of race.

Those in attendance had come to the nation's capital from across the country and from all walks of life. They were blacks and whites; doctors, lawyers, and common folk; rich and poor. It was a festive and historic occasion.

Martin Luther King Jr.—the same minister who had organized the African Americans' boycott of buses in Montgomery, Alabama, after the Rosa Parks incident—delivered one of the most famous speeches in history on that day in Washington, DC. It became known as his "I Have a Dream" speech. It spoke of King's vision for America and his hope for a day when everyone would be treated equally, regardless of the color of his or her skin.

Most people considered the march a rousing success. But Malcolm X was not like most people. Although he, like King, was among the most prominent civil rights leaders in America and stood to benefit from the

The March on Washington, DC, the event at which Martin Luther King Jr. delivered his "I Have a Dream" speech, was held on August 28, 1963.

gathering, Malcolm did not support it. He called it the "Farce on Washington" and said it could not really be successful because it was too peaceful and there were too many white people there. He said the whites "engulfed it. They became so much a part of it [that] it lost its original flavor. It ceased to be angry. It ceased to be impatient. In fact, it ceased to be a march. It became a picnic."[1]

Malcolm never had been a fan of King, whose philosophy of blacks and whites living together in harmony greatly differed from Malcolm's philosophy of separating the races. Though their tactics may have differed, each man had his legion of followers. But when Malcolm criticized the harmonious March on Washington, many blacks began to wonder what Malcolm's motives really were. After an event that occurred that fall, they would question them even more.

Growing Tensions

When President John F. Kennedy was assassinated in November 1963, in Dallas, Texas, Elijah Muhammad ordered Malcolm and all other members of the Nation of Islam not to comment on the president's death. Kennedy was a very popular president, even among African Americans, and the entire country was saddened by his death. However, Malcolm did not follow his leader's orders. He told one reporter that the president's killing was a case of "the chickens coming home to roost,"[2] meaning that Kennedy was somehow responsible for his own death. Malcolm added, smiling, "Chickens coming home to roost never did make me sad; they've always made me glad."[3]

Martin Luther King Jr. and Malcolm X met in person in
Washington, DC, on March 26, 1964.

Malcolm later said his comments about Kennedy's assassination were taken out of context. He said, "I said the hate in white men had not stopped with the killing of defenseless black people, but that hate, allowed to spread unchecked, finally had struck down this country's Chief of State."[4]

Muhammad did not see any humor in Malcolm's comments, which ran the following day in newspapers all across the country. He summoned Malcolm to Chicago to meet with him and suspended Malcolm from the Nation of Islam for a period of time. Publicly, Malcolm appeared to be fine with Muhammad's decision, even saying at times that he felt he deserved it. But deep down, the suspension angered Malcolm and signaled the beginning of the end of his involvement with Muhammad and the Nation of Islam.

To take his mind off his situation and to get out of New York—where members of his own temple had begun speaking out against him and where he was not allowed to speak—Malcolm headed to Miami, Florida. A young boxer named Cassius Clay was there training for a big fight against heavyweight champion Sonny Liston and had invited Malcolm to come watch him train and to help him mentally prepare for the fight. Clay was a Black Muslim and had known Malcolm for a couple of years.

Malcolm was ringside on February 25, the day of the fight. The bigger and older Liston was heavily favored to beat Clay, but, prior to the fight, Malcolm gave Clay a pep talk. Eventually, the outspoken Clay defied the odds to become the heavyweight champion of the world. The day

"THE GREATEST"

After his bike was stolen, twelve-year-old Cassius Clay made quite an impression on a local police officer: He told the cop he wanted to beat up the thief. By chance, the policeman also was a

(continued on the next page)

Boxing champion Muhammad Ali, a converted Muslim, and Malcolm X became friends in the 1960s.

(continued from the previous page)

a boxing trainer and offered to teach the sport to the angry boy. Clay was a talented student, and eventually won a gold medal in boxing in the 1960 Olympics. He became a professional boxer shortly thereafter, earned the nickname "The Greatest," changed his name to Muhammad Ali, and became the world champion in 1964, though his pro career was tinged with controversy. His biggest controversy came in 1967 when Ali, who was a recently converted Black Muslim, refused to serve in the US military during the Vietnam War. Ali said his religion would not allow him to fight. Ali's refusal angered many Americans and the government found Ali guilty of refusing induction into the military. He appealed and eventually cleared his name but he lost his boxing title and the sport banned him from competition for three-and-a-half years. Ali returned to the ring following the ban, eventually retiring from boxing in 1981. He died on June 3, 2016.

after the fight, Clay announced to the world that he was a Muslim, which he had been for a while, and that he had changed his name to Muhammad Ali.

The time he spent with Ali may have provided a much-needed break for Malcolm, but all it did was delay what seemed to be an inevitable outcome: Malcolm was going to break away from the Nation of Islam. In March, he did just that. Malcolm held a press conference announcing that he was resigning from the Nation of Islam. He said he believed it was time for him to start a movement of his own. He named his new Islamic organization Muslim Mosque, Inc. It was to be a religious and political organization.

The split with the Nation of Islam also destroyed Malcolm's relationship with Muhammad Ali, although Malcolm would not readily admit that his good friend had broken off their friendship. Malcolm said on the record that he did not believe Ali had made any negative statements about him, even though Ali did several times.

Malcolm said members of his Muslim Mosque also could continue being members of the Nation of Islam if they wanted to. But that was before he began hearing rumors that the Nation of Islam was plotting to have him killed.

On March 26, Malcolm met Martin Luther King Jr. for the first and last time. Though the two civil rights leaders had been known to disagree with each other's methodology, the meeting appeared to be cordial. King had just finished debating civil rights legislation in Washington, DC, when Malcolm met him. The two men shook hands, and most of the photos taken of the meeting show both men wearing wide smiles.

When Malcolm split with the Nation of Islam, he had to forfeit all the possessions the Nation owned. That included his house, his car, and the money the group was paying him. Malcolm did not give up the house he and his family were living in without a fight, which he took to court and eventually lost. Before he did, however, Malcolm's refusal to turn the home over to the Nation of Islam angered its members.

Malcolm's exit from the Nation of Islam left him nearly broke, and it placed a severe damper on the next plan he hoped to execute. However, with financial help from his sister, Malcolm was able to make his desired pilgrimage to Mecca, Saudi Arabia. The trip, called a hajj, is mandatory for all adult Muslims who can afford it and are healthy enough to make it. Mecca is considered the center of the Muslim religion. It is the birthplace of the Prophet Muhammad and of Islam, the religion he started thirteen hundred years prior to Malcolm's trip.

Pilgrimage to Mecca

For more than a month, Malcolm toured the Middle East and Africa. He was

All adult Muslims who can afford to do so are encouraged to make a pilgrimage to Mecca, Saudi Arabia. Malcolm X made the trip, and was amazed to see Muslims of all skin colors, not just blacks.

fascinated with what he saw. Mecca was full of Muslims of all skin colors, not just blacks. In Mecca, all Muslims were treated equally. Everyone was united for the same purposes: to worship and respect their god, Allah, and to practice peace and unity. During his time there, Malcolm sent a postcard home to author Alex Haley, who had been interviewing Malcolm and helping him write his autobiography. The postcard said Malcolm had "eaten from the same plate with fellow Muslims whose eyes were bluer than blue, whose hair was blond, blonder than blond, whose skin was whiter than white ... And we were all the same."[5]

Malcolm told another friend that Mecca had changed his narrow-minded way of thinking. Despite all the years he had spent preaching it, Malcolm's trip to Mecca made him realize all white men were not devils, after all. Malcolm learned that the traditional religion of Islam was different from what Muhammad had taught him. Malcolm returned to America a changed man, although he still did not believe blacks and whites should integrate. Malcolm also had a different name. The man who had been born Malcolm Little, and then had become Malcolm X, had changed his name again, this time to the traditional Muslim name of Hajj Malik El-Shabazz. Most people, however, continued to refer to him as Malcolm X.

His trip to Mecca was a successful venture for Malcolm, but his recently founded Muslim Mosque was not. He had a hard time recruiting members. He did not abandon the organization, but he did decide to start another one. He called this one the Organization of Afro-American Unity (OAAU). The OAAU called on blacks to control all their own institutions, and promised to help them do so. The first OAAU meeting was held June 28, 1964, in New York. The speech Malcolm gave on that day became one of his most famous of all time. He said, in part:

> *We don't care how rough it is. We don't care how tough it is. We don't care how backward it may sound. In essence it only means we want one thing. We declare our right on this earth to be a man, to be a human being, to be respected as a human being, to be given the rights of a human being in this society, on this earth, in this day, which we intend to bring into existence by any means necessary.*[6]

Malcolm's Enemies

Malcolm's departure from the Nation of Islam—and the many negative things he had said about its leader, Elijah Muhammad—had left him with many enemies. The newspaper he claimed he helped found, *Muhammad Speaks*, began running negative articles about him. The paper once reported: "Only those who wish to be led to hell, or to their doom, will follow Malcolm. The die is set, and Malcolm shall not escape."[7] Malcolm believed this to be true and interpreted it to mean that his split with Islam probably would end with his own violent death.

Many people grew to hate Malcolm, and he began receiving death threats. Black Muslims constantly drove by his house. Malcolm's wife, Betty, said the people driving by were vicious. Even though Malcolm no longer believed

Malcolm X poses for a photo in 1963, holding newspapers that contain articles about him.

that his followers should carry weapons, he bought a gun for his house, taught Betty how to use it, and told her to shoot anyone who tried to come through their door. Malcolm often called the police, and sometimes he was granted police protection. FBI files from the time show that Malcolm was indeed being harassed.

The threats of harm, which regularly occurred even when Malcolm was conducting interviews, did not deter him from his mission of promoting the OAAU. He encouraged blacks to take part in the political process and to become active in their communities. He gave speeches, appeared on talk-radio programs, and granted interviews to dozens of magazines and newspapers. He even traveled to Africa to meet with the leaders of several countries to try to gain their support. He wanted to put pressure on the United Nations to reprimand the United States for its treatment of blacks.

The irony was that because Malcolm spent such a long time in Africa, the OAAU and the nearly defunct Muslim Mosque suffered from lack of leadership. Not many blacks were willing to follow the "new" Malcolm.

Sixty of his followers greeted Malcolm at the airport when he returned to the United States on November 24, 1964. He picked up right where he had left off, promoting his mission of black equality. In February 1965, Malcolm and Martin Luther King Jr. took their respective civil rights battles to Selma, Alabama. At the time, blacks in the South still were struggling with certain civil rights, including the ability to vote in some elections. A campaign for black voting rights was being held in Selma. King was already in jail when Malcolm arrived in town, having been arrested during a protest on February 2. King recently had won the Nobel Peace Prize, and was more popular than ever, with every move he made being reported on by the press. It would be logical to think that Malcolm would be happy that a fellow black man had been given one of the most prestigious honors given to a person and had used that honor to help spread his message of equality for blacks. But Malcolm was not happy because he felt King had not been effective in solving the problem of racial discrimination.

Malcolm had come to Selma because he was invited by an activist organization to speak. Before he took the stage, many of those in the audience feared Malcolm's rebellious words might start a riot. But, in fact, his speech talked about how blacks needed to come together for the common good. He told the media he believed any effort to give black people the right to vote was a good thing, even if it came from King.

The next day, Malcolm hopped a plane to London, where he spoke at the First Congress of the Council of

African Organizations. Then he left for Paris, where he was to speak to the Federation of African Students. When Malcolm's plane landed there, French authorities took him into custody and would not let him enter their country. No official reason was given, but author Bruce Perry said the officials "hinted that the U.S. State Department had asked them to bar him from France."[8]

A news story on the incident ran in the (London) *Times*. It read: "Malcolm X, the American Negro militant leader, was refused entry to France this morning and ordered to return to London. The decision to refuse him entry was taken on the grounds that his presence could disturb public order."[9] Malcolm was quoted in the article as saying, "The authorities would not even let me contact the American Embassy. I was shocked. I thought I was in South Africa. I did not even get as far as immigration control. They took me to a room where I was kept in seclusion by three policemen. I might as well have been locked up. They would not let me speak to anyone or telephone."[10]

Whatever the reason, Malcolm was placed on the next plane to London. On February 13, he flew back to New York. Malcolm believed something dreadful would eventually happen to him, but he had no idea when. As it turned out, that misfortune was waiting for him when he got home.

6

"They're Killing My Husband"

Malcolm, his wife, and their four children were asleep when destruction hit their New York home. It was shortly after 2:30 a.m. on February 14, 1965, after all, and Malcolm had just returned from a long, stressful trip overseas. Nevertheless, all six people in the household abruptly awoke at almost the same time, after Malcolm heard the sound of broken glass. Shortly after, he noticed his living room was on fire—someone had tossed a firebomb through a window. Malcolm and Betty rushed their children outside. Malcolm then went back inside the brick house to retrieve some personal belongings. His wife, who was pregnant at the time of the fire, later talked about how she was impressed with her husband's courage in the face of danger. Betty said, "I always knew he was strong, but at that hour I realized how great his strength was."[1]

Malcolm, Betty, and their four young girls stood outside in the cold winter night and watched as their house burned. It was the second time in his life Malcolm had stood by and watched as flames destroyed the place he called home. The first time, he was a young child. This time, he was a man.

Though no one was ever charged with the crime, Malcolm believed he knew who was to blame for the firebombing and let the media know it the next day. He claimed his house was bombed by the Black Muslim movement under orders from Elijah Muhammad.

For its part, the Nation of Islam denied any wrong-doing. In fact, one of its leaders, Joseph X, said he believed Malcolm himself had started the fire "to get publicity."[2] He told one newspaper, "We own the place. He was going to be evicted. Why would we bomb our own property?"[3]

Although it may sound ridiculous that Malcolm would set fire to his own home—especially with his wife and children inside—it is not that far-fetched of a theory. Malcolm was about to lose the house anyway, so what did he have to lose by setting the fire, as long as he knew for sure he could get his family out before they were harmed? At least then, the Nation of Islam could not have it, either. Malcolm strongly denied he played any role in the fire, though. Just as they had in 1929 when young Malcolm's house had burned to the ground, questions surrounded the cause of this blaze.

"If anybody can find where I bombed my own house they can put a bullet through my head."[4]

After the fire, Malcolm's wife and children went to stay at a friend's house. Malcolm did not go with them. He spent the next few hours preparing to catch a plane to Detroit, where he was scheduled to speak. When he arrived at his hotel in Detroit, Malcolm was still visibly shaken from what had happened to him

Malcolm X gets out of his car at his house, which had been firebombed the previous evening, on February 15, 1965.

and his family. He was given a sedative by a doctor. It is easy to understand why Malcolm would appear shaken. In addition to the fire, the threats against his life recently had intensified. In one incident, described by the ghostwriter of his autobiography, Alex Haley, Malcolm was involved in a car chase in Los Angeles that could have turned deadly. A car, driven by a member of the Nation of Islam, tried to run Malcolm's car off the road.

Now, with the fire at his home, even his family appeared to be at risk. Malcolm continued to tell anyone who would listen how he believed he was a marked man. He said he expected to be killed, but the unsettling thing was that he never knew when it was going to come.

Malcolm stood true to his word and continued to work. On February 15, he was back in New York, speaking to a crowd of six hundred people at the Audubon Ballroom at a rally for his Organization for Afro-American Unity. According to the FBI, Malcolm talked

Malcolm X giving one of his many speeches in New York City on June 28, 1964.

about the firebombs that had hit his home and accused the Nation of Islam of doing it. Then, he "claimed that a conspiracy exists between the NOI [Nation of Islam] and the Ku Klux Klan that is not in the best interest of the black people. He alleged that the NOI and the Klan have agreed to leave each other alone and that the Klan has offered land in North Carolina to the NOI for the latter's 'separate state' for Negroes plan."[5]

For the time being, Malcolm decided to remain separated from his family to keep them safe, and he checked into a hotel. He and Betty did go looking for a house of their own, however. They even agreed to put the home in someone else's name to help keep their lives anonymous. Author Russell J. Rickford said that Malcolm was trying to save his relationship with his wife by spending more time with her. His frequent traveling had put a strain on his marriage.

The Audubon Ballroom

But before he could fully clear his calendar, Malcolm had some more big speeches to get through. Following a speech at Columbia University in New York, Malcolm's next speech was scheduled for February 21, back at the Audubon Ballroom in Harlem, where he had talked just six days earlier at an OAAU rally. The day before the February 21 speech, Malcolm called Haley to tell him he had some doubts as to whether it was indeed the Nation of Islam that was after him. He did not say who he thought might be harassing him.

On the morning of February 21, Malcolm called his wife from his hotel room and asked her if she would

The Audubon Ballroom in Harlem, New York, is where Malcolm X was assassinated on February 21, 1965.

get the children dressed and bring them to the Audubon Ballroom to hear him speak that afternoon. She agreed to do so, although she was surprised he had asked; he had told her earlier that she should stay home because he did not think it would be safe for her to attend.

Most of the ballroom's four hundred seats were filled by the time Betty and her four daughters arrived at the venue, but they found a few open seats in the front row. Most of the crowd were members of Malcolm's Organization for Afro-American Unity, there to hear another inspirational message from their charismatic leader.

Malcolm smiled during his introduction and began to speak. He said, *As-salaam alaikum.* Peace be with you. The crowd responded back: *Wa-alaikum salaam.* And peace be with you. Malcolm then noticed a commotion a few rows back in the audience. He looked out into the crowd, and said, "Let's cool it, brothers."[6] Those would be his last words. Seconds later, a shotgun blast ripped through the wooden podium Malcolm was standing behind, hitting him in the chest and knocking him backward over two empty chairs. Malcolm fell to the ground. The shotgun fired again. Someone then tossed a smoke bomb inside the ballroom. Two black men then jumped from their seats, pulled out their pistols, and began firing into Malcolm's prone body.

One of Malcolm's bodyguards shot one of the gunmen in the leg as he tried to flee. The man kept going, making it outside, where he was beaten by the crowd that had followed him out. Police had to stop the people from killing the gunman. The man turned out to be a twenty-two-year-old black man named Talmadge Hayer. Eyewitness reports from the scene said there were possibly four or five total assassins, but they all safely escaped.

Inside the ballroom, Malcolm's pregnant wife had thrown her daughters to the floor and shielded them with her body. When the shooting began, she screamed, "They're killing my husband!"[7] On stage, a few people gathered around Malcolm, who was bloodied and motionless. One woman who said she was a registered nurse said, "I rushed to the stage even while the firing was going on. I don't know how I got on the stage, but I threw myself down on who I thought was Malcolm— but it wasn't. I was willing to die for the man. I would have taken the bullets myself. Then I saw Malcolm, and the firing had stopped, and I tried to give him artificial respiration. I think he was dead then."[8]

Meanwhile, several of Malcolm's supporters rushed across the street to a hospital, took a stretcher, and

AN ALL-OUT WAR?

Police and civil rights leaders feared Malcolm's death might start an all-out war between his followers and the followers of Elijah Muhammad. That never transpired, although there were some isolated incidents. For example, the day after Malcolm was killed, a firebomb was thrown through a fourth-floor window at the Nation of Islam's Temple Seven, the Harlem mosque where Malcolm had once been leader. Six firefighters were hurt battling the blaze, which destroyed the building. Police had been standing guard outside, but no one was seen committing the crime. Bomb threats also were called in across the city of New York. One Harlem newspaper ran an editorial on its front page hoping to help stop a riot from occurring.

brought it back for Malcolm. They wheeled him out of the venue and to the hospital. A famous photograph taken at the time shows Malcolm lying on a stretcher, being escorted by several police officers.

But it was too late. The thirty-nine-year-old black leader—admitted to the hospital under the name "John Doe" because no one had yet officially identified him—was dead on arrival. An autopsy showed that

Many shops in Harlem were temporarily closed in honor of Malcolm X on the day of his funeral, and long lines of people waited outside the funeral home to attend his service.

Malcolm died of pellets from a shotgun and bullets from two different pistols, a .45 caliber and a 9 mm. News of Malcolm's death spread quickly.

That Malcolm had touched an enormous number of lives became apparent shortly after his death. Tens of thousands of mourners poured into the Unity Funeral Home in Harlem to view Malcolm's open casket. The line into the funeral home extended for blocks. Viewing had to be stopped several times while police searched for bombs.

Many Harlem shops were shuttered for a period in tribute to Malcolm. Many stores also closed for Malcolm's funeral service, which was held Saturday, February 27, at the Faith Temple Church of God. As could be expected, security at the church was tight, with hundreds of uniformed police officers on hand. The church was filled to capacity, and thousands of people who could not get in stood by outside. After the service, Malcolm was taken to Ferncliff

Cemetery outside New York City in Hartsdale, where he was buried under the name Hajj Malik El-Shabazz, the name he had taken after his trip to Mecca.

Investigation, Arrests, and Trials

By the time their investigation was complete, police had arrested three members of the Nation of Islam, charging each one with the murder of Malcolm X. The police settled on just those three suspects even though eyewitnesses had said there were up to five assassins. Investigators also thought there likely were more people involved. But in the end, the men charged with Malcolm's murder were Hayer, who had been arrested at the scene; Norman 3X Butler; and Thomas 15X Johnson. Their trial began on January 12, 1966, in New York City.

The prosecution had a strong case against Hayer. After all, he was the one who had been seen fleeing the scene of the crime, was shot by a bodyguard, and then mauled by the crowd until police arrived to arrest him. When they did so, they found a bullet that matched the murder weapon in his pocket. But the case against the other two defendants was not as strong. There was no physical evidence against them, as there had been for Hayer. The only real evidence against Butler and Johnson was eyewitness testimony, and even that proved shaky at best.

Six weeks into the trial, after long claiming his innocence, Hayer took the stand and told everyone he had shot Malcolm. Hayer said someone had hired him to kill Malcolm, but he would not say who.

The jury was not swayed by Hayer's sudden change of opinion. After deliberating for more than twenty hours, it found all three men guilty of first-degree murder, meaning they faced mandatory sentences of life in prison. Three men were in prison for Malcolm's murder, but there still were many unanswered questions about what had happened inside the Audubon Ballroom on February 21, 1965. Those unanswered questions would be the source of many debates for decades to come.

7

A Lasting Legacy

Millions of people bought *The Autobiography of Malcolm X* upon its release a few months after Malcolm's death. The book—written with the help of ghostwriter Alex Haley—became required reading in schools, even though some historians believe many of the events described in the book were embellished to suit Malcolm's agenda. The autobiography mainly focused on African Americans' long struggle for civil rights. Still, the battle for civil rights for black people continued to be fought long after Malcolm's death.

Perhaps the best-known civil rights leader ever, and one of Malcolm's chief rivals, Martin Luther King Jr., suffered a fate similar to Malcolm's a few years later. On April 4, 1968, King was in Memphis, Tennessee, to lead a protest march for that city's black garbage workers, who were on strike. Standing on the balcony of his hotel room in the early evening hours, King was shot in the neck. He died a short time later at the hospital. The death of King—who always had preached against violent acts—was followed by riots in several cities. A white convict named James Earl Ray was convicted of

The Autobiography of Malcolm X, written with the help of ghostwriter Alex Haley, was published a few months after Malcolm's death.

THE AUTOBIOGRAPHY OF
MALCOLM X

King's murder and sentenced to ninety-nine years in prison, where he died in 1998 at the age of seventy.

Over the years, other people who fought for civil rights also have died tragically. One, white presidential candidate Robert Kennedy, younger brother of assassinated president John F. Kennedy, was shot and killed in June 1968, just two months after King's murder.

Shortly after Malcolm's death, a group called the Black Panther Party was formed. The Black Panthers were a political organization that promoted a radical, pro-black agenda. Many of its members—and many police officers and innocent bystanders—were killed in violent acts attributed to the Black Panthers.

In November 1965, Betty Shabazz gave birth to twin girls, Malaak and Malikah. After Malcolm's death, the grieving widow received thousands of cards, letters, and phone calls telling her how great a man her husband was. Thanks to the donations and fund-raising efforts of Malcolm's friends and supporters, Betty and her daughters were able to purchase a large house in Mount Vernon, New York. Over the years, Malcolm's widow often lectured at colleges across the country and spoke at gatherings for certain organizations. Oftentimes, her pro-black messages sounded just like her deceased husband's. She also spoke out for women's rights.

The Nation of Islam continued under the leadership of Elijah Muhammad, until his death in 1975 at the age of seventy-seven. That is when Muhammad's son, Wallace, took over the organization, renamed it, and made several changes. The changes angered some members of the Nation and caused many of them to leave the group. One of those departing members,

Many people, including Malcom X's wife, Betty, believed that the Nation of Islam minister Louis Farrakhan had something to do with the murder of Malcolm X.

Louis Farrakhan, took the Nation of Islam name for his new group, which followed many of the same guidelines as Muhammad's group had.

Family Troubles

The charismatic Farrakhan soon became the focus of Betty Shabazz's attention. Betty began saying she believed Farrakhan played a role in her husband's death. In 1994, her second daughter, thirty-four-year-old Qubilah, was arrested for conspiring to murder Farrakhan, whom she believed played a main role in her father's killing. Qubilah made a deal with prosecutors, who allowed her to avoid going to trial if she sought psychiatric counseling, and she agreed to drug and alcohol treatment. In an unexpected move, Farrakhan issued a public statement saying he forgave Qubilah. A few months later, Betty met Farrakhan on stage at Harlem's Apollo Theater, where they shook hands in a show of peace.

The family trouble did not end with Qubilah's arrest. In June 1997, Qubilah's twelve-year-old son, named Malcolm after the grandfather he never knew, set fire to his grandmother's apartment in Yonkers, New York. Betty Shabazz suffered burns on more than 80 percent of her body during the fire. She died three weeks later at the age of sixty-one. She is buried next to her husband at Ferncliff Cemetery. Thousands of people visit the modest burial site each year.

In June 1997, Betty Shabazz's grandson set a fire in her apartment. She died

CREATING HER OWN LEGACY

Betty Shabazz struggled to cope with her husband Malcolm's assassination, but her resolve soon was strengthened by her own spiritual pilgrimage to Mecca. After the visit, she continued to raise her six daughters alone while simultaneously managing to earn a doctorate from the University of Massachusetts. She then went to work at Medgar Evers College in Brooklyn, New York. A private person by nature, Shabazz felt she had a duty as wife of one of the best-known black men of all time and helped carry on her husband's legacy and his work whenever she could. She played a key role in the renaming of one of the City Colleges of Chicago to Malcolm X College and worked tirelessly to maintain control over the use of her husband's name, while using it herself when necessary in her ongoing work to help underprivileged children. Her work was not overlooked. Following her untimely death in 1997, many American leaders released statements paying tribute to Shabazz, including then-President Bill Clinton and the Reverend Jesse Jackson. More than two thousand people attended her memorial service, including poet Maya Angelou and the governor of New

(continued on the next page)

(continued from the previous page)

York. Today, several tributes stand as testaments to her life's work, including the Malcolm X and Dr. Betty Shabazz Memorial and Educational Center and the Dr. Betty Shabazz Health Center, both in New York, and the Betty Shabazz International Charter School in Chicago, Illinois.

several days later after suffering burns over more than 80 percent of her body.

Shortly after the death of Elijah Muhammad, one of the men convicted of killing Malcolm changed the confession he had made at the trial, and he offered another version of what had happened to Malcolm. Talmadge Hayer said he was recruited to kill Malcolm by two members of the Nation of Islam because the Nation felt Malcolm had betrayed them. Hayer wrote at the time: "I thought it was very bad for anyone to go against the teaching of the Hon. Elijah, then known as the last Messenger of God. I was told that Muslims should more or less be willing to fight against hypocrites and I agreed [with] that. There was no money payed [sic] to me for my part in this."[1] Hayer again said that his codefendants, Norman 3X Butler and Thomas 15X Johnson, had nothing to do with the crime.

Hayer's revised story had little effect on his or anyone else's situation, and all three men remained behind bars. They all changed their names to Muslim names, and eventually they were paroled from prison. In another strange irony, Butler became head of the Nation of Islam's Temple Seven after his release. The person he was found guilty of killing had transformed the same temple from a storefront in the ghetto into the Nation of Islam's most powerful branch.

CONCLUSION

Today, all across the United States, there are countless memorials and monuments commemorating the life of Malcolm X. The site of his childhood home in Omaha, Nebraska, is listed on the National Register of Historic Places. The house Malcolm lived in there has since been torn down, but the property is owned and maintained by a nonprofit group called the Malcolm X Memorial Foundation. Located just off Malcolm X Avenue, the property has a large sign that reads "Malcolm X Birth Site" and another that tells his life story and ends with the words, "His teaching lives on." A similar sign exists in Lansing, Michigan. In cities across the country, there are also numerous streets and schools named after Malcolm. Even the site of his death has become a shrine of sorts. The Audubon Ballroom in Harlem is now home to the Malcolm X and Dr. Betty Shabazz Memorial and Educational Center. Highlights of the center include rare photos, videos, documents, and more.

In 1992, a major motion picture, simply titled *Malcolm X*, was released. The film, directed by Spike Lee, was a box-office smash. Actor Denzel Washington portrayed Malcolm, and actress Angela Bassett played the role of his wife, Betty. Washington won several awards for his portrayal, and he was nominated for a highly coveted Best Actor Academy Award. The plot of the film drew heavily from *The Autobiography of Malcolm X*.

The exact details of Malcolm X's death likely will never be known. Did orders for his death come from Elijah Muhammad, Louis Farrakhan, or another of the higher-ups in the Nation of Islam? Most historians agree that the Black Muslims were in some way responsible for Malcolm's death, but what role did particular people play in the 1965 shooting at the Audubon Ballroom in Harlem?

Throughout much of his adult life, Malcolm had talked about how he believed he would not live long enough to see old age, but he rarely mentioned what he hoped his legacy might be. Six weeks before he was murdered, he finally discussed that very subject. A newspaper reporter named Claude Lewis prompted the discussion, asking Malcolm how he would like to be remembered. Malcolm quickly answered: "Sincere. In whatever I did or do, even if I make mistakes, they were made in sincerity. If I'm wrong, I'm wrong in sincerity. I think that the best a person can be—he can be wrong, but if he's sincere you can put up with him. But you can't put up with a person who's right, if he's insincere."[1]

Malcolm X was not an actor, but he played many roles during the thirty-nine years he was alive. He was the son of an outspoken black man, and he was a petty criminal jailed for his crimes. He was a loyal husband, a loving father, and a spiritual leader empowered with an eloquent speaking ability that could captivate an audience. In each of these roles, he achieved the goal he told Lewis he wanted to achieve. In each of these roles, Malcolm X was indeed sincere.

CHRONOLOGY

1925   Malcolm Little is born on May 19 to Earl
and Louise Little.

1929   The Little family home in Lansing,
Michigan, burns to the ground.

1931   Malcolm begins kindergarten;
Earl Little dies.

1939   Louise Little is declared legally insane and
is committed to Kalamazoo State Mental
Hospital in Michigan; Malcolm is sent to a
juvenile detention home.

1941   Malcolm moves to Boston, Massachusetts,
to live with his half sister Ella; he works
various jobs, including on the railroad.

1942   He moves back to Michigan for a short
period of time and then returns to Boston.

1943   He moves to Harlem, New York; he gains
the nickname "Detroit Red"; he is found
"mentally disqualified" for military service.

1946   Malcolm is arrested attempting to pick
up a stolen watch he had left at a jewelry
store; he is sentenced to eight to ten years
in prison.

1949   He converts to the Nation of Islam religion;
he begins to follow the teachings of
Elijah Muhammad.

1952   He is paroled from prison at the age of
twenty-seven; he gets a job at a Detroit
furniture store.

1953   Malcolm becomes the assistant minister
of the Nation of Islam temple in Detroit; he

changes his name from Malcolm Little to Malcolm X; he founds and becomes minister of the first Nation of Islam temple in Boston.

1954 He becomes the acting minister of the Philadelphia, Pennsylvania, temple; he becomes minister of the New York temple.

1955 He becomes the minister of Philadelphia temple; Rosa Parks makes a stand on the bus in Montgomery, Alabama.

1957 Malcolm becomes the minister of the Detroit temple.

1958 He marries fellow Black Muslim Betty X; their daughter Attallah is born.

1959 Malcolm appears in the television documentary *The Hate That Hate Produced*; he travels to the Middle East and Africa as the National of Islam's ambassador.

1960 He meets with Cuban leader Fidel Castro in Harlem, New York; daughter Qubilah is born.

1961 He helps found the Nation of Islam newspaper *Muhammad Speaks*.

1962 He becomes the Nation of Islam's national minister; daughter Ilyasah is born; he flies to Los Angeles, California, to calm the crowd after the death of Nation of Islam member Ronald Stokes.

1963 The March on Washington, DC, takes place; Malcolm ignites controversy and is suspended by the Nation of Islam over some comments made about the death of President John F. Kennedy.

1964 Malcolm leaves the Nation of Islam and forms his own group, Muslim Mosque Inc.; he travels to Mecca, Saudi Arabia; he changes name to Hajj Malik El-Shabazz.

1965 His family home in New York is firebombed; he is assassinated on February 21; twins Malaak and Malikah are born; *The Autobiography of Malcolm X* is published.

CHAPTER NOTES

Introduction

1. Alex Haley and Malcolm X, *The Autobiography of Malcolm X* (New York: Ballantine Books, 1992), p. 3.

2. Ibid.

3. Ibid.

4. Bruce Perry, *Malcolm X: The Life of a Black Man Who Changed Black America* (Barrytown, NY: Station Hill Press, Inc., 1991), p. 9.

5. Perry, p. 10.

6. Kofi Natambu, *The Life and Work of Malcolm X* (Indianapolis, IN: Alpha Books, 2001), p. 4.

Chapter 1: On the Move

1. Bruce Perry, *Malcolm X: The Life of a Black Man Who Changed Black America* (Barrytown, NY: Station Hill Press, Inc., 1991), p. 3.

2. Perry, pp. 3–4.

3. Perry, p. 10.

4. Alex Haley and Malcolm X, *The Autobiography of Malcolm X* (New York: Ballantine Books, 1992), p. 14.

5. Haley and Malcolm X p. 21.

6. David Gallen, *Malcolm X: As They Knew Him* (New York: Carroll and Graf, 1992), p. 122.

7. Perry, p. 39.

Chapter 2: Growing Up on the Streets

1. Rodnell P. Collins with A. Peter Bailey, *Seventh Child: A Family Memoir of Malcolm X* (Seacaucus, NJ: Birch Lane Press, 1998), p. 209.

2. David Gallen, *Malcolm X: As They Knew Him* (New York: Carroll and Graf, 1992), pp. 121–122.

3. Gallen, p. 123.

4. "The Harlem Riot 1943," TheHistoryBox.com, http://www.thehistorybox.com/ny_city/riots /SectionIII/riots_article7a.htm.

5. Ibid.

6. Haley and Malcolm X, p. 110.

Chapter 3: A New Name

1. Rodnell P. Collins with A. Peter Bailey, *Seventh Child: A Family Memoir of Malcolm X* (Seacaucus, NJ: Birch Lane Press, 1998), p. 70.

2. Michael Eric Dyson, *Making Malcolm: The Myth and Meaning of Malcolm X* (New York: Oxford University Press, 1995), p. 6.

3. Alex Haley and Malcolm X, *The Autobiography of Malcolm X* (New York: Ballantine Books, 1992), p. 164.

4. Bruce Perry, *Malcolm X: The Life of a Black Man Who Changed Black America* (Barrytown, NY: Station Hill Press, Inc., 1991), p. 118.

5. Perry, p. 144.

6. Perry, pp. 144–145.

7. Haley and Malcolm X, p. 203.

8. Perry, p. 164.

9. Ibid.

10. Haley and Malcolm X, p. 238.

Chapter 4: Spreading the Word

1. "Transcript of Malcolm X Weekly Column in Los Angeles *Herald-Dispatch*," November 21, 1957, reproduced on *Malcolm X: The FBI Files*, April 2004, http://www.wonderwheel.net/work /foia/1958/021758-043058/articles/112157lahd.pdf.

2. "Death and Transfiguration," *Time*, March 5, 1965, http://www.time.com/time/magazine /article/0,9171,839291-3,00.html

3. "Malcolm X: Make It Plain Transcript," PBS.org, May 19, 2005, http://www.pbs.org/wgbh/amex /malcolmx/filmmore/pt.html.

4. Ibid.

5. Ibid.

6. Ibid.

Chapter 5: Leaving the Nation of Islam

1. Bruce Perry, *Malcolm X: The Life of a Black Man Who Changed Black America* (Barrytown, NY: Station Hill Press, Inc., 1991), p. 211.

2. Perry, p. 241.

3. Ibid.

4. Alex Haley and Malcolm X, *The Autobiography of Malcolm X* (New York: Ballantine Books, 1992), p. 307.

5. David Gallen, *Malcolm X: As They Knew Him* (New York: Carroll and Graf, 1992), p. 71.

6. Malcolm X, "Speech on the Founding of the O.A.A.U.," June 28, 1964, reproduced on BlackPast.org, http://www.blackpast.org/1964-malcolm-x-s-speech-founding-rally-organization-afro-american-unity.

7. "Death and Transfiguration," *Time*, March 5, 1965, http://www.time.com/time/magazine/article/0,9171,839291-4,00.html.

8. Perry, p. 351.

9. "Malcolm X Barred," *Times* (London), February 10, 1965, p. B-11, reproduced on Center for Contemporary Black History (Columbia University), http://www.columbia.edu/cu/ccbh/mxp/images/sourcebook_img_161.jpg.

10. Ibid.

Chapter 6: "They're Killing My Husband"

1. Russell J. Rickford, *Betty Shabazz: A Remarkable Story of Survival and Faith Before and After Malcolm X* (Naperville, Ill.: Sourcebooks, Inc., 2003), p. 223.

2. "Malcolm Accuses Muslims of Blaze; They Point to Him," *New York Times*, February 16, 1965, reproduced on *Center for Contemporary Black History* (Columbia University), http://www.columbia.edu/cu/ccbh/mxp/images/sourcebook_img_163.jpg

3. "Malcolm X Denies He Is Bomber," *Amsterdam News*, February 20, 1965, reproduced on *Center for Contemporary Black History* (Columbia University), http://www.columbia.edu/cu/ccbh/mxp/images/sourcebook_img_165.jpg.

4. Ibid.

5. Clayborne Carson, *Malcolm X: The FBI File* (New York: Carroll and Graf, 1991), p. 357.

6. Rickford, p. 229.

7. Ibid.

8. Peter Kihss, "Malcolm X Shot to Death at Rally Here," *New York Times*, February 22, 1965, reproduced on *Center for Contemporary Black History* (Columbia University), http://www.columbia.edu/cu/ccbh/mxp/images/sourcebook_img_169.jpg.

Chapter 7: A Lasting Legacy

1. Michael Friedly, *Malcolm X: The Assassination* (New York: Carrol and Graf, 1992), p. 85.

Conclusion

1. David Gallen, *Malcolm X: As They Knew Him*, (New York: Carroll and Graf, 1992) p. 177.

GLOSSARY

bigoted Intolerant of any race, creed, or opinion that differs from one's own.

boycott To abstain from using.

charisma A particularly strong appeal or charm.

Communist An adherent of Communism, a system of government in which a single political party controls goods and services.

deed A usually sealed written document containing a contract.

deport To expel from a country.

dictatorship A type of government where one person is in complete control.

discrepancies Differences or inconsistencies.

divisive Creating a division between two things.

hypocrisy Pretending to believe something when one truly believes the opposite.

illegitimate Born to parents who were not married to each other.

integration Combining or uniting two or more parts.

jurisdiction The power to exercise authority over something or someone.

methodology The way one works toward a goal; procedure.

militia A group of citizens organized to fight for certain rights, but not part of the regular army.

mosque A place of public worship used by Muslims.

nationalism A strong feeling of devotion to one's own country.

persecution Punishment or harassment of a group or individual based on race, religion, or political beliefs.

propaganda Facts or ideas spread to help further one's own cause or to damage another's cause.

propagate To spread among people.

prophecy A prediction of the future.

regime A mode of rule or management.

temperament The emotional qualities and personality traits of a person.

FURTHER READING

Books

King, Martin Luther Jr. and Walter Dean Myers. *A Time to Break Silence: The Essential Works of Martin Luther King, Jr., For Students.* Boston: Beacon Press, 2013.

Malcolm X. *Malcolm X Speaks: Selected Speeches and Statements.* New York: Grove Press, 1965.

Nelson, Kadir. *Heart and Soul: The Story of America and African Americans.* New York: Balzer + Bray, 2013.

Parks, Rosa. *Rosa Parks: My Story.* New York: Puffin Books, 1992.

Shabazz, Ilyasah. *Malcolm Little: The Boy Who Grew Up to Become Malcolm X.* New York: Atheneum Books, 2013.

Sheinkin, Steve. *The Port Chicago 50: Disaster, Mutiny, and the Fight for Civil Rights.* New York, Roaring Brook Press, 2014.

Websites

African American Odyssey: A Quest for Full Citizenship

memory.loc.gov/ammem/aaohtml/exhibit/aointro.html

Includes more than 240 African-American-related items from the collections from the Library of Congress.

The Civil Rights Movement

www.cnn.com/EVENTS/1997/mlk/links.html

This chronological history of the important events of the American civil rights movement includes links to stories on other civil rights pioneers, including Rosa Parks, the National Civil Rights Movement, and the NAACP.

The Malcolm X and Dr. Betty Shabazz Memorial and Education Center

theshabazzcenter.net

Located in New York City, The Malcolm X and Dr. Betty Shabazz Memorial and Education Center is a memorial to these civil rights activists. Upcoming events, a photo gallery, and a video gallery are all included on this website.

Malcolm X Official Site

www.malcolmx.com

The official site includes photos, Malcolm's famous quotes, news, and a store featuring Malcolm-related goods. It also includes biographical information about Malcolm X, as well as general information about the civil rights movement.

Marcus Garvey Tribute

http://marcusgarvey.com

This website features several speeches, poems, and philosophical beliefs of the Jamaican-born black nationalist who had a strong influence on the life of Malcolm X's parents.

The Martin Luther King Jr. Center for Nonviolent Change

www.thekingcenter.org

Established in 1968, The Martin Luther King Jr. Center for Nonviolent Change is headquartered in Atlanta, Georgia. This, the center's website, offers extensive information on King's life, with a goal of creating a "living memorial filled with all the vitality that was [King's], a center of human endeavor, committed to the causes for which [King] lived and died."

Films

Malcolm X, 1992

The award-winning Malcolm X biopic based on his own autobiography.

Selma, 2014

An award-winning historical drama detailing Martin Luther King Jr.'s march from Selma, Alabama, in 1965.

INDEX